# You CAN Try This At Home!

Diana Noonan

Photography by
Lindsay Edwards

## Contents

# You Be the Scientist

Hi there! My name is Robbie, and this is Ella. We love science! We love to learn about the world and how it works. So we do lots of **experiments**.

You don't need lots of equipment to be a **scientist** – you can do these fun experiments in your own home!

Let's go!

Make sure you ask a grown-up for permission first!

# Disco Fruit

Are you ready to make dried fruit dance? Sounds weird doesn't it? But it's really easy and a lot of fun!

Here's what you need:

- some dried fruit
- baking soda
- white vinegar
- a glass.

Here's what to do:

1. Fill the glass with hot water, until it is ¾ full.
2. Stir in 2 big tablespoons of baking soda until it **dissolves**.

3 Drop some dried fruit into the glass.

4 Pour in 3 big tablespoons of vinegar.

Mixing vinegar with baking soda makes a gas. You can see the gas as the bubbles that fizz up. The bubbles stick to the fruit and lift it up. When the bubbles reach the top of the water, they burst. Then, the fruit drops to the bottom. This happens over and over again, and it looks like the fruit is dancing!

# The Rubbery Egg

Did you know that you can make an egg shell soft? Well, you can! You can make an egg shell turn rubbery!

Here's what you need:

- an egg
- white vinegar
- a glass.

Here's what to do:

1. Place the egg carefully in the glass.
2. Pour some vinegar into the glass, making sure the egg is fully covered.

3. Leave the egg in the vinegar for three days.

4. Take the egg out of the vinegar. Wash the egg in cold water.

Vinegar is an acid.
**Acid** can make some things dissolve, or wear away.

The acid in the vinegar makes the egg shell wear away. But the egg's skin is still strong enough to stop the egg from falling apart.

# The Ice Lifter

How would you like to lift an ice cube with a piece of thread? Come on, let's do it!

Here's what you need:

- an ice cube
- a piece of sewing thread
- a teaspoon of salt.

Here's what to do:

1. Put the ice cube on a table or plate.
2. Put the thread across the ice cube.
3. Lift the thread off the ice cube. The ice cube doesn't move.

4 Put the thread across the ice cube again.

5 Pour the salt onto the ice cube so that it covers the thread.

6 Wait a few seconds.

7 Now, take hold of each end of the thread and lift up the ice cube!

The salt melts the ice on the top of the ice cube, making a small puddle of water. The rest of the ice cube is still very cold, so the water quickly freezes again around the thread. The thread is now stuck to the ice. So, an ice cube **can** be lifted with a piece of thread!

# The Noisy Fork

When you think about noisy things, I bet you don't think about forks! But I'll show you how loud a fork can be!

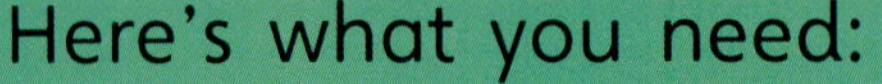

Here's what you need:

- a metal fork
- a piece of string about one metre long
- a chair.

Here's what to do:

1. Tie the middle of the string to the handle of the fork.
2. Wind an end of the string around each of your pointer fingers.

3. Hit the chair with the fork. It's not very loud, is it?
4. Now put your pointer fingers carefully in your ears. Don't untie the string!

5
Bend over and bump the fork against the chair again.
Wow! When the fork hits the chair, it sounds like loud bells! How come?

When you hear a sound, it travels to your ears through the air. When you hit the chair with the fork the first time, the sound travelled through the air. The sound went in all directions around the room. You could also hear lots of other sounds at the same time.

When you hit the chair with the fork the second time, you had your fingers in your ears. The sound of the fork travelled straight up the string to your ears. Because you had your fingers in your ears, you could only hear the sound from the fork. It sounded much louder – like bells!

# The Magic Balloon

Now let's blow up a balloon without blowing into it! Sounds impossible doesn't it? Read on!

Here's what you need:

- a balloon
- a small plastic bottle
- 6 tablespoons of white vinegar
- 2 tablespoons of baking soda.

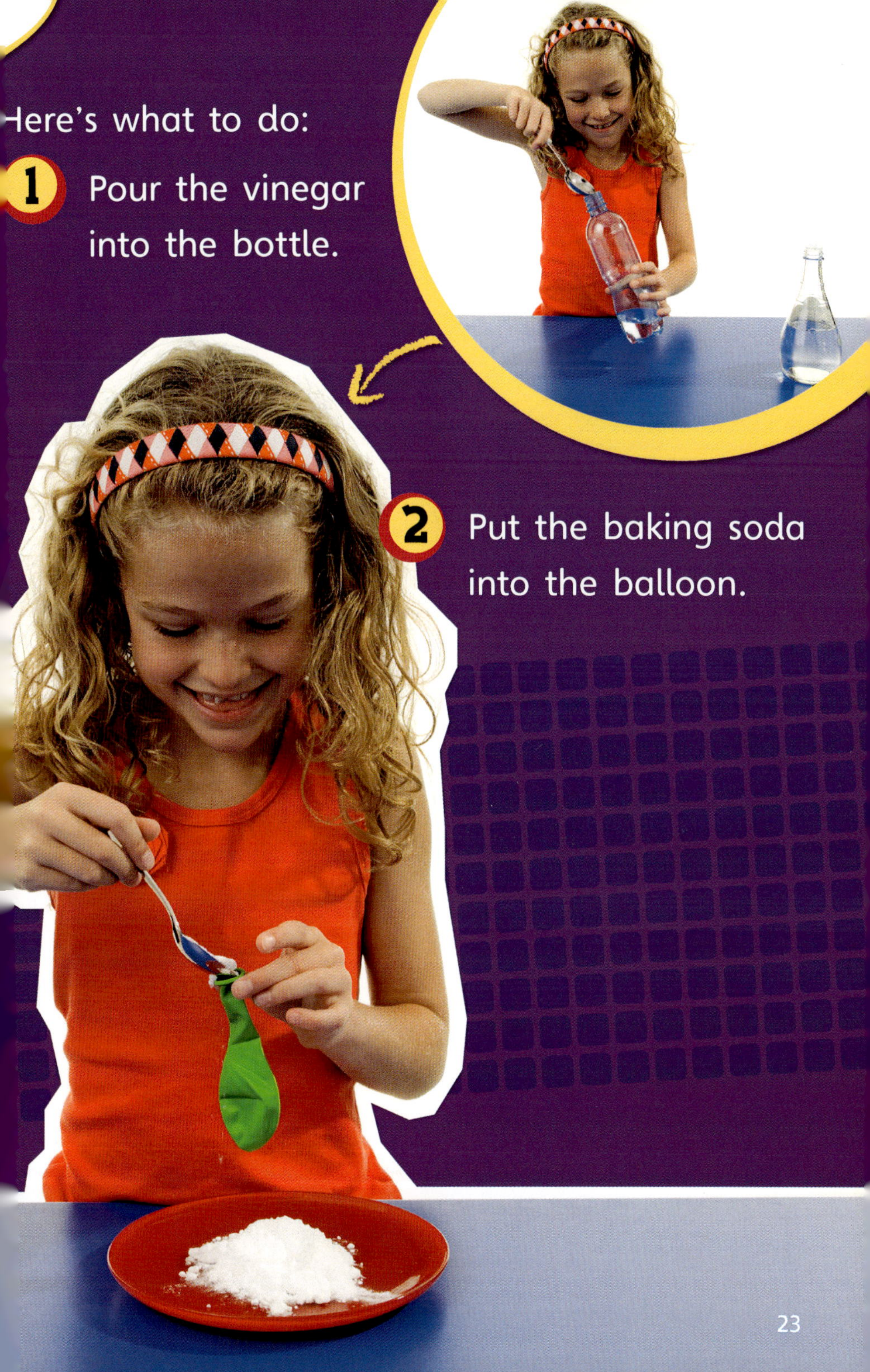

Here's what to do:

1 Pour the vinegar into the bottle.

2 Put the baking soda into the balloon.

3. Put the balloon over the top of the bottle.
4. Lift the balloon so that the baking soda falls into the bottle.

When the vinegar and baking soda are mixed together, they make a gas. The gas rises to the top of the bottle. The gas goes into the balloon and it blows up!

# Potato or Apple?

I love apples! I like potatoes! But how do I know that I like apples more than potatoes? Is it just by tasting them? Or, does looking at and smelling food also play a part?

Here's what you need:

- a slice of apple
- a slice of **raw** potato
- a peeler.

Here's what to do:

1. First, peel the slices of apple and potato. Ask a grown-up to help.

2. Close your eyes.

3. Mix up the two slices so you don't know which slice is which.

4 Hold your nose and eat each piece.

Your nose and mouth share the same airway. So you taste and smell at the same time.

Your **sense** of taste tells you if food tastes salty, sweet or sour. Your sense of smell adds to your sense of taste. If you also close your eyes, your brain finds it hard to tell the difference between a potato and an apple!

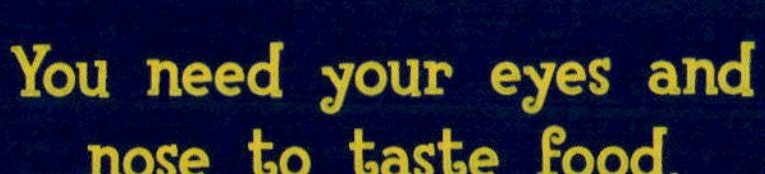

You need your eyes and nose to taste food.

# You Can Do It Too!

So you see, science can be easy – and fun, to
You don't have to work in a **laboratory**. You c
be a scientist using everyday things at home.

Have fun trying thes
experiments. There is
whole world of scien
for you to explore!

Go on – you CAN do it!

# Glossary

**acid** a liquid that can eat away at things

**dissolves** to disappear into a liquid

**experiments** activities that help people understand scientific ideas

**laboratory** a place with chemicals and special instruments where scientists do tests on things

**raw** not cooked

**scientist** someone who studies science

**sense** any one of the five ways that your body finds out about thing The senses are sight, hearing, smell, taste and touch.